The Developing

Artist

PIANO SONATINAS
Book Two   Intermediate

A COMPREHENSIVE,
WELL-GRADED SERIES
OF AUTHENTIC
KEYBOARD SONATINAS

T0057120

Compiled and edited by
Nancy and Randall Faber

Production: Frank & Gail Hackinson
Production Coordinator: Marilyn Cole
Cover: Terpstra Design, San Francisco
Engraving: GrayBear Music Company, Hollywood, Florida
Printer: Vicks

FABER
PIANO ADVENTURES

ISBN 978-1-61677-111-9

TABLE OF CONTENTS

The table of contents is listed alphabetically by composer. The selections in the book, however, are presented in approximate order of difficulty.

UNDERSTANDING MUSICAL FORM

Musical *form* is a way of organizing or structuring music.

Composers of sonatas and sonatinas (little sonatas) have written hundreds of pieces with new and different themes (melodies). However, composers usually used only a few musical forms over and over to give structure to their compositions. Imagine a baker baking hundreds of different cakes, but always using the same set of cake pans. Similarly, a composer can create many different pieces using a single musical form.

The following forms are common in early-level classical sonatinas. You and your teacher may wish to refer to this page as you study the sonatinas in this book.

Binary (2-part) form or AB form

The simplest musical form is one section of music followed by another: **section A** followed by **section B.** Each section usually has a repeat sign.
This 2-part (binary) form can be shown like this:

For example: *Sonatina* by Diabelli (page 14)

Rounded binary form

This is still 2-part form, but with an interesting feature. In rounded binary form, the theme from section **A** returns *within* the **B** section.
It can be shown like this:

$$\|\!: \ \textbf{A} \ :\|\!: \ \textbf{B} \ (\text{A}) \ :\| \quad \text{(coda optional)}$$

For example: 1st movement from *Sonatina in C* by Haslinger (page 16)

Ternary (3-part) form or ABA form

Ternary means 3-parts: **section A, section B,** and the return of **section A.** Ternary form is common in slow, lyric second movements.
This 3-part form can be shown like this:

A B A (coda optional)

For example: *Minuetto* from *Sonatina Op.39, No.1* by Lynes (page 28)

Rondo form

In this form, the **A section** reappears after each new section.
Rondo form is common for lively third movements.
A typical rondo form looks like this:

A B A C A (coda optional)

For example: *Vivace* from *Sonatina Op.55, No.1* by Kuhlau (page 58)

Sonata-allegro form

A more complex form called **sonata-allegro form** is used for first movements of sonatas and longer sonatinas. Many sonatinas, however, vary from precisely following the form.

In the first section, called the **exposition**, the themes are presented or "exposed."
The 1st theme is usually followed by a more lyrical 2nd theme, usually in the key of the dominant (scale step 5). The exposition may end with a closing theme.
The entire exposition is usually repeated.

The middle section is called the **development**. Themes or parts of themes may be presented in new keys or "developed" in imaginative ways. Shorter sonatinas may have only a transitional passage instead of a development section.

The final section is called the **recapitulation**. Here the themes are restated, or "recapped." Both the 1st and 2nd themes appear in the tonic key.

A *coda* (ending) or *codetta* (short ending) will often end the movement.

Sonata-allegro form can be shown like this:

Exposition	Development	Recapitulation (coda)
1st theme	(themes developed and accidentals appear due to key changes)	**1st theme** (in the tonic)
2nd theme (in the dominant)		**2nd theme** (in the tonic)
closing theme (optional)		closing theme (in the tonic)

For example: *Allegro* from *Sonatina Op.55, No.1* by Kuhlau (page 55)

Sonatina in G

Ludwig van Beethoven
(1770-1827)

Moderato

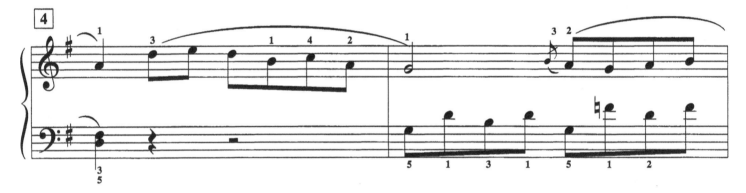

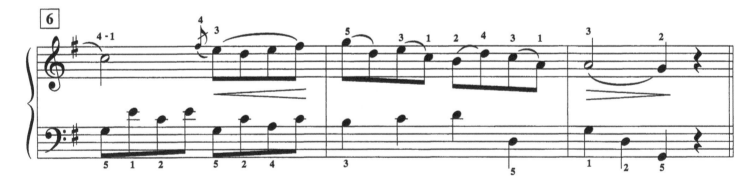

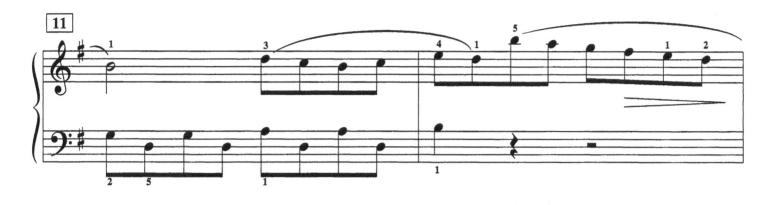

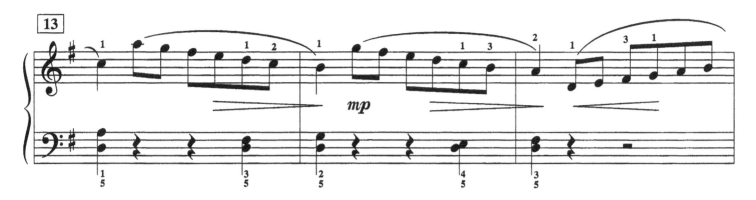

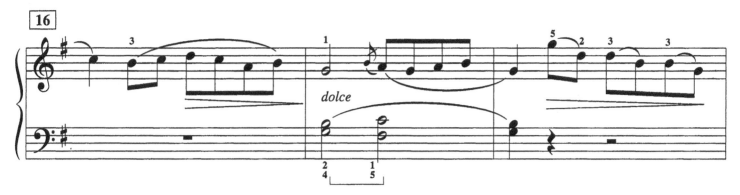

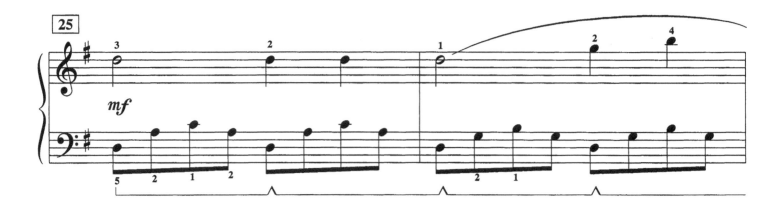

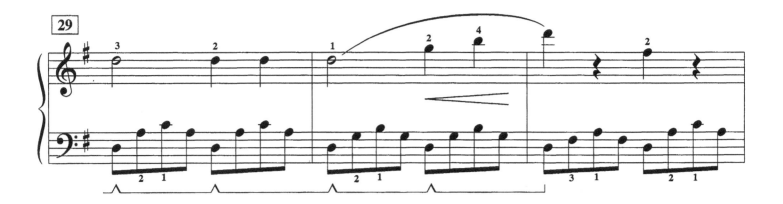

Exploring the Score: Beethoven often composed long *codas* (endings) to his music.

This sonatina has an **A section, B section,** return of the **A section,** and a long **coda**.

• With the help of your teacher, find each section in your music.

II

Romanze

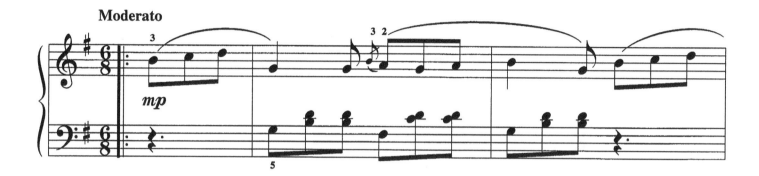

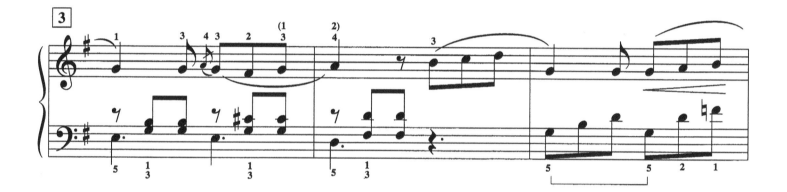

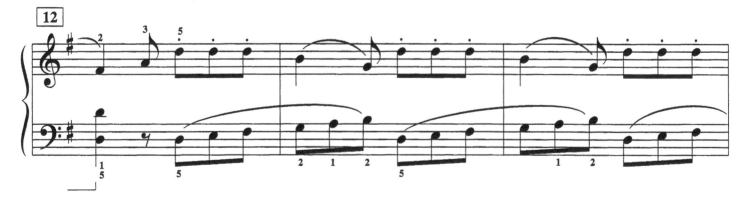

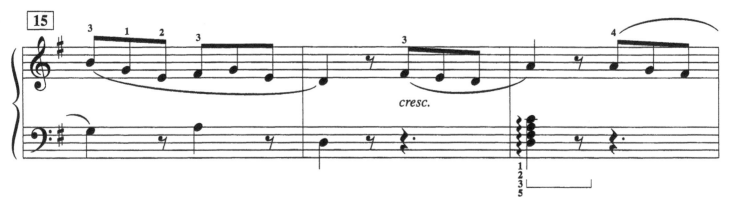

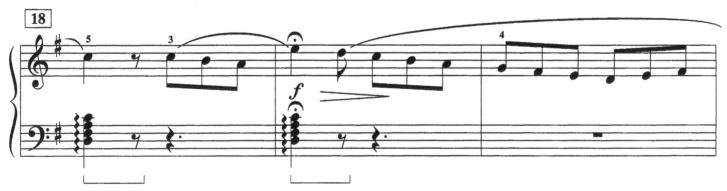

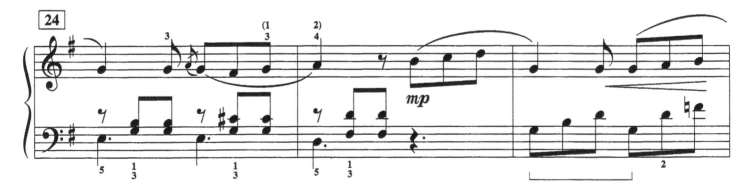

Exploring the Score: An ending section is called a **coda**.

$\|: \text{ A } :\|: \text{ B } (\text{A}) :\|$ coda

- With the help of your teacher, label **section A, section B** and the **coda** in your music.

- Where does the opening theme return within section B?

Sonatina in C
(1st Movement)

Jean T. Latour
(1766-1837)

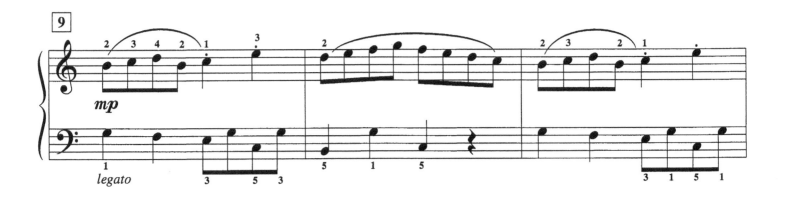

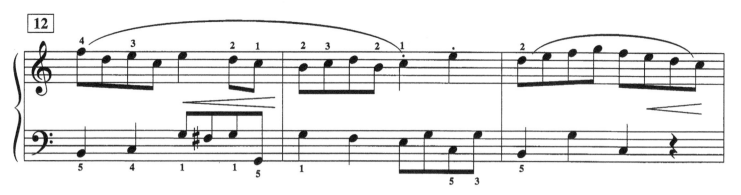

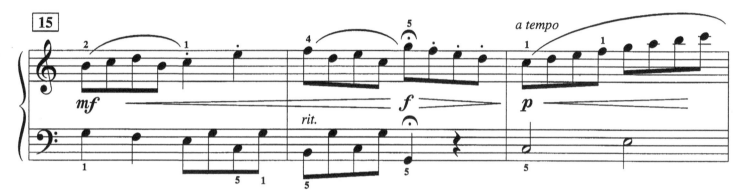

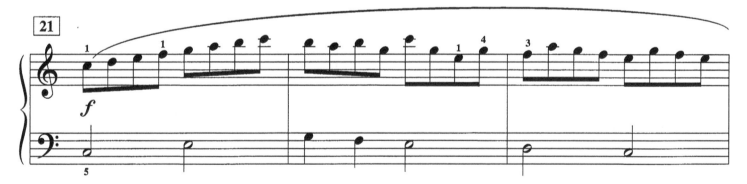

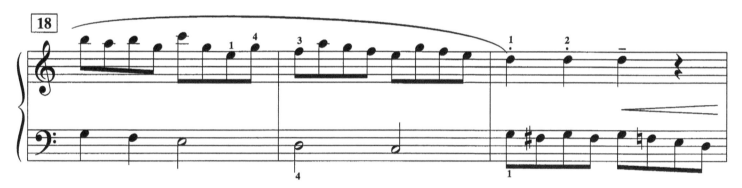

Exploring the Score: By using a fermata in measure 16, the composer Latour creates suspense for which upcoming section? *(circle one)*

the coda   B Section   return of the A Section

Sonatina in F
(1st Movement)

Anton Diabelli
(1781-1858)

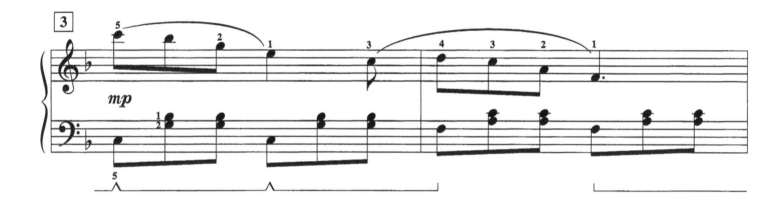

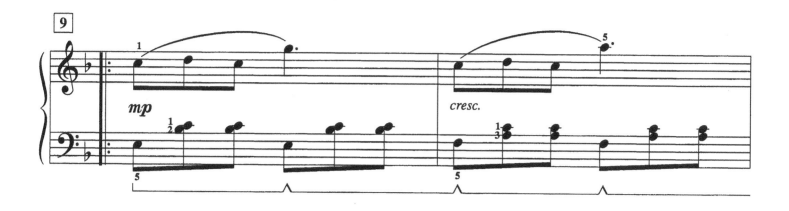

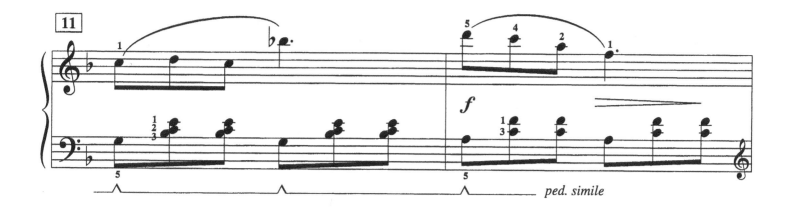

Exploring the Score: Circle the form of this movement:

Binary   Rounded binary   Ternary

‖: A :‖: B :‖   ‖: A :‖: B (A) :‖   A B A

Sonatina in C

Tobias Haslinger
(1787-1842)

Allegro non tanto

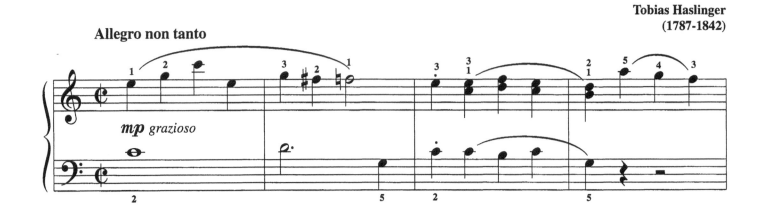

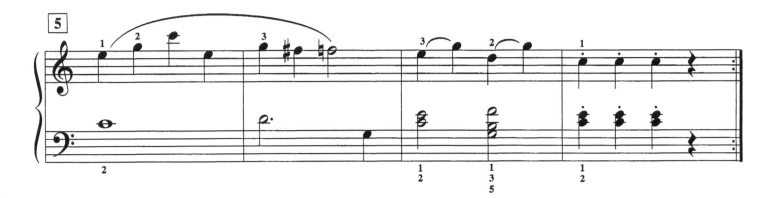

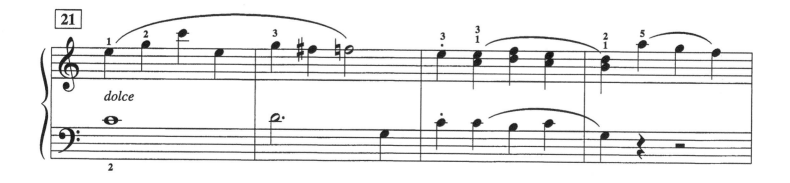

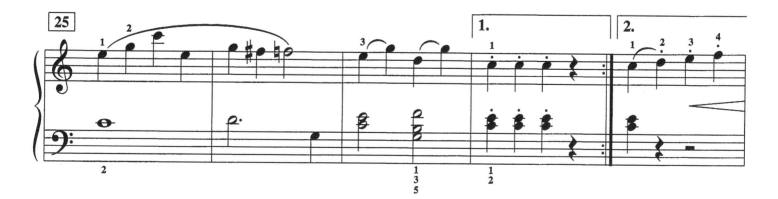

Exploring the Score: A short *coda* is called a *codetta*.

- Is the ending of this piece a *coda* or a *codetta*?

- Is the form of this piece **binary** or **rounded binary**? *(circle one)*

II

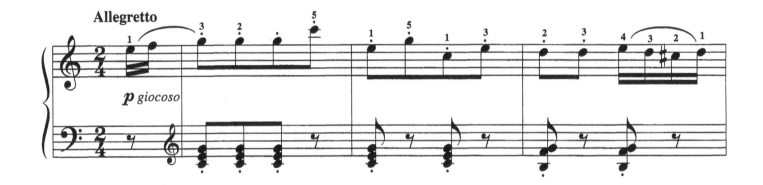

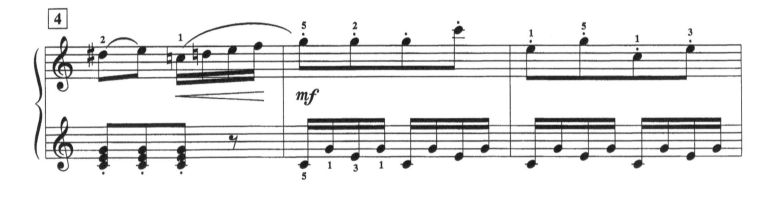

Exploring the Score: Circle the form of this movement:

Binary with coda   Rounded binary with coda   Ternary with coda

‖: **A** :‖‖: **B** :‖ coda   ‖: **A** :‖‖: **B** (A) :‖ coda   **A B A**   coda

Sonatina in F

Thomas Attwood
(1765-1838)

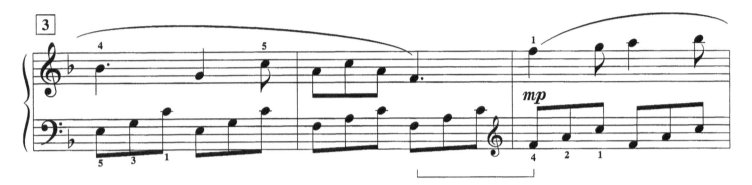

Exploring the Score: A passage which connects two sections is called a **transition**.

- Can you find the transition in this piece?

- Circle the correct form:

‖: **A** :‖: *transition* **B A** :‖   or   ‖: **A** :‖ **B** *transition* **A** :‖

II

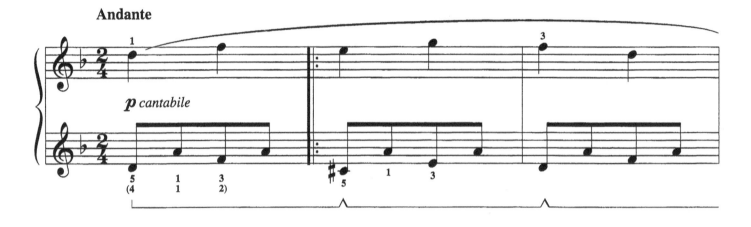

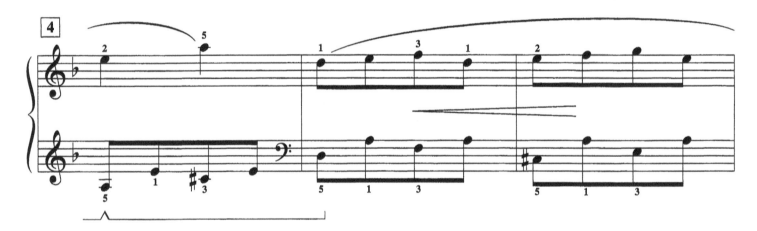

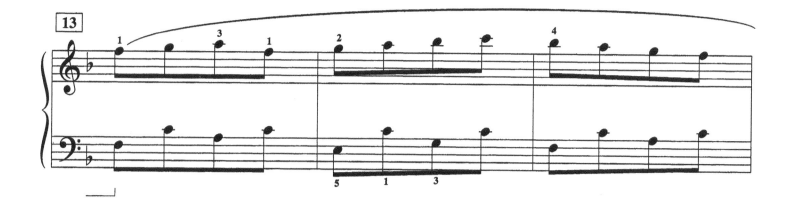

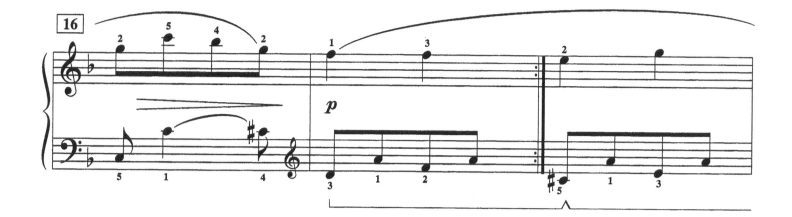

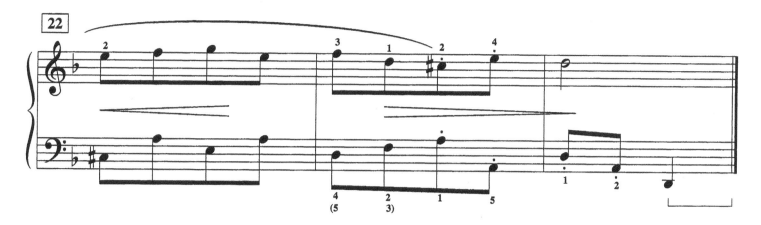

Exploring the Score: Where does the opening theme appear in a major key? *measure* ___

Name the key: ___ major.

III

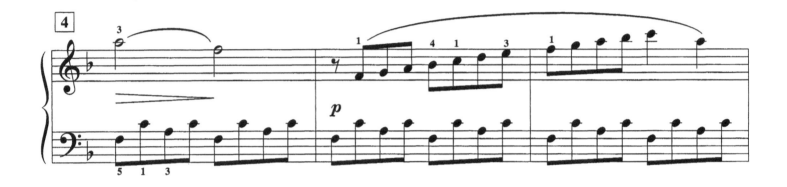

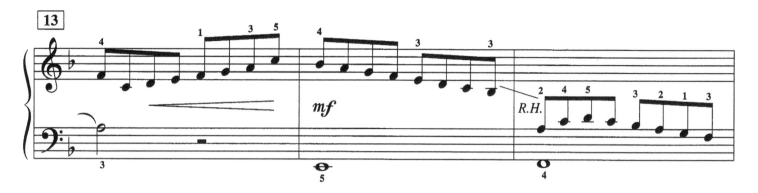

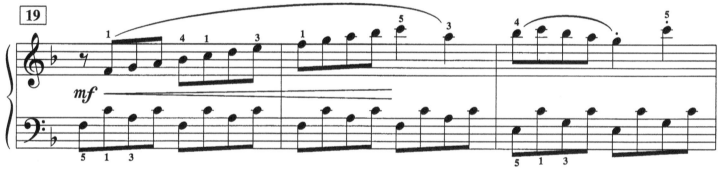

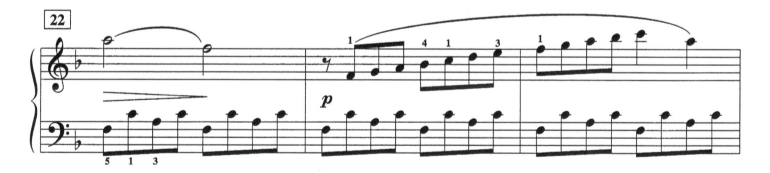

Exploring the Score:

- Is the right hand in this movement based on *scales* or the *Alberti bass?* (circle one)

- Does the left hand use *scales* or the *Alberti bass?* (circle one)

Sonatina
Op. 39, No. 1

Frank Lynes
(1853-1913)

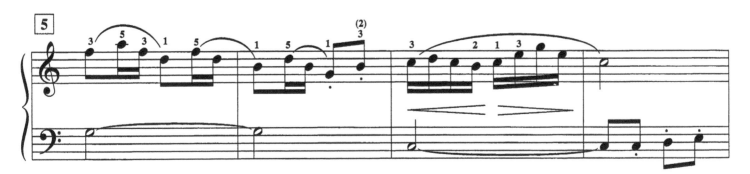

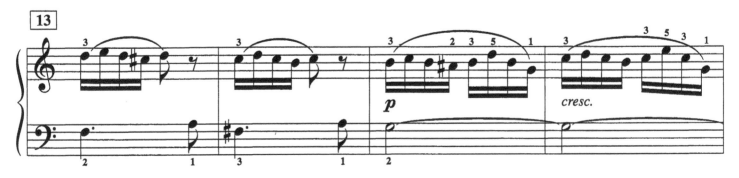

Exploring the Score: Remember, a passage which connects two sections is called a **transition**.

- Can you find the 4-measure transition which leads to the return of the opening theme?

II

Minuetto

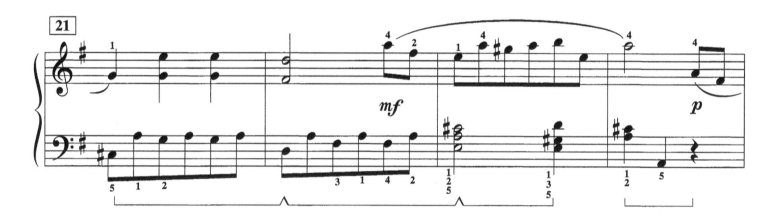

30

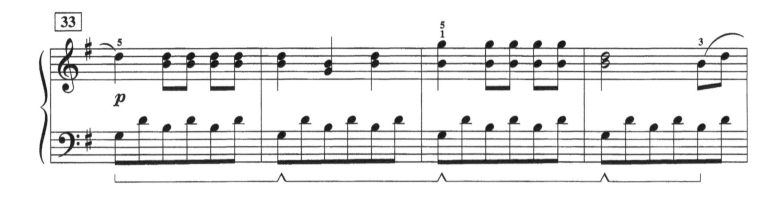

Exploring the Score: Circle the form of this movement:

A B A   A B coda   A B A B

III

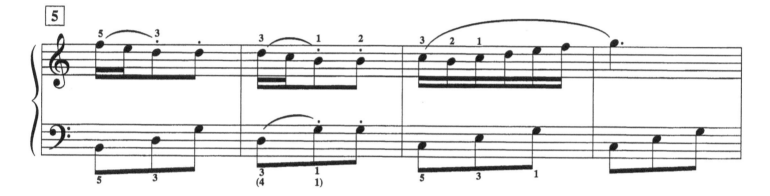

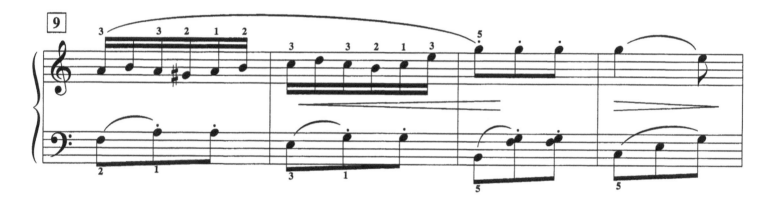

32

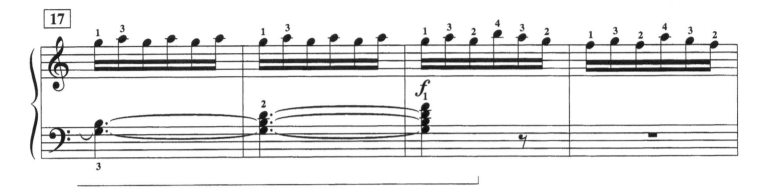

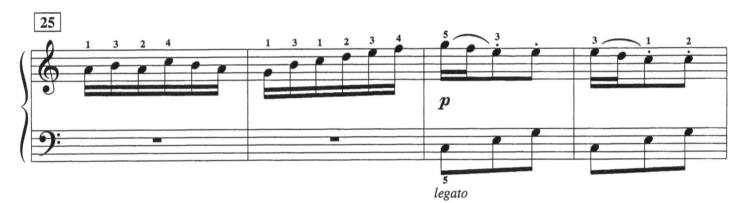

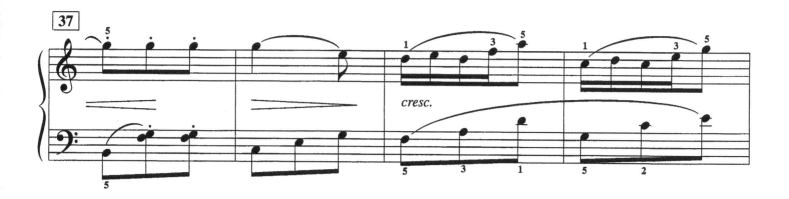

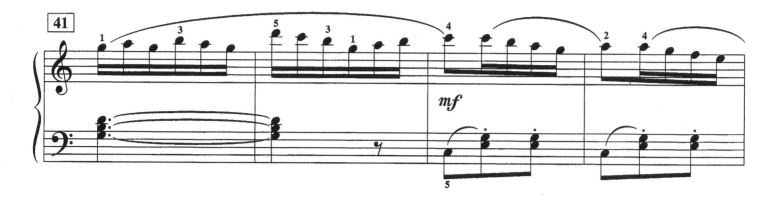

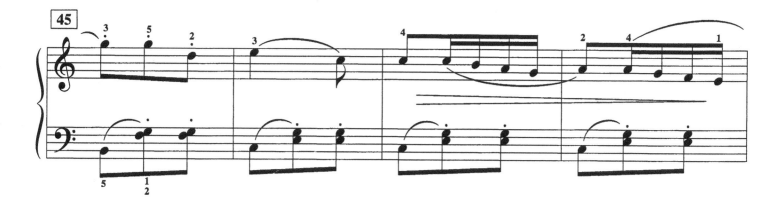

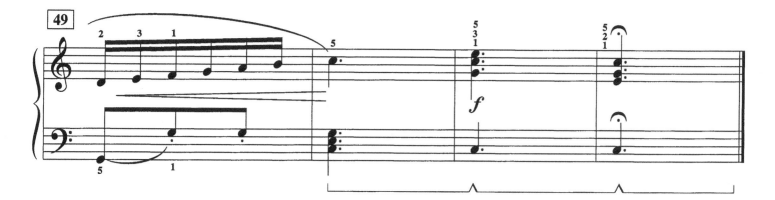

Exploring the Score: This movement has a long, showy transition.

- Where does the transition begin?

- Where does the opening theme return?

Sonatina
Op. 36, No. 1

Muzio Clementi
(1752-1832)

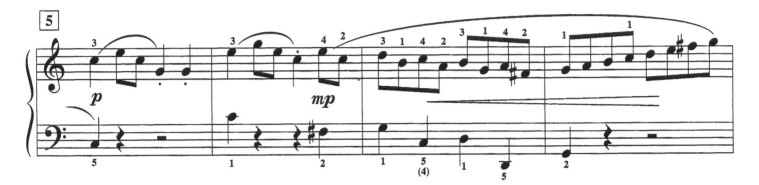

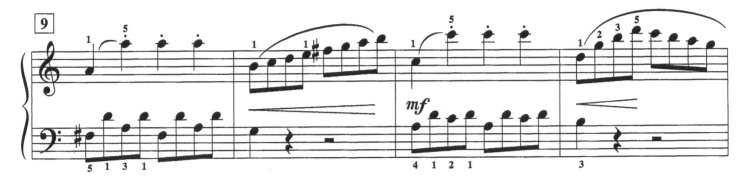

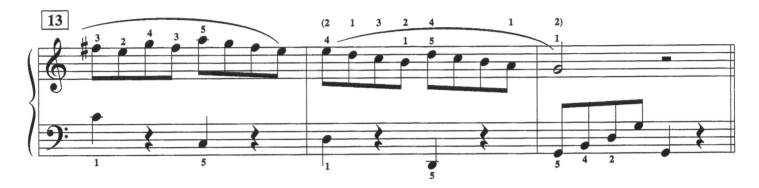

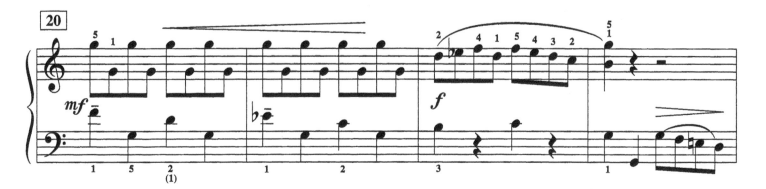

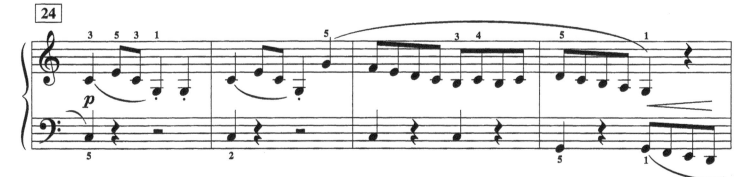

Exploring the Score: This movement is in sonata-allegro form. Study "sonata-allegro" form on page 5
with the help of your teacher. Then label the following in your music:

Exposition   **Development**   **Recapitulation**

• Can you find the 1st and 2nd theme in the exposition? In the "recap"?

II

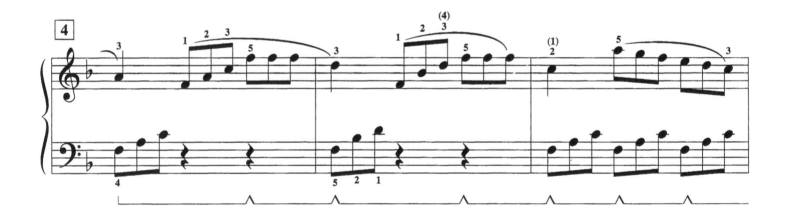

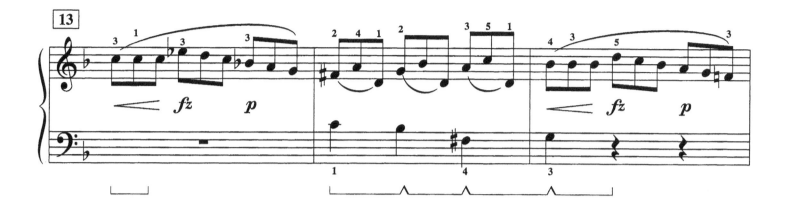

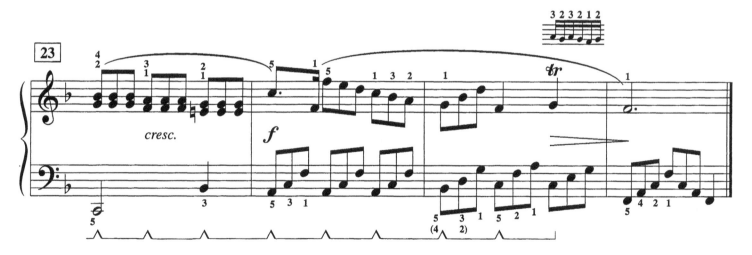

Exploring the Score:

- Where does the opening theme return? *measure* ___

- On what note does the melody change in the return? ___

III

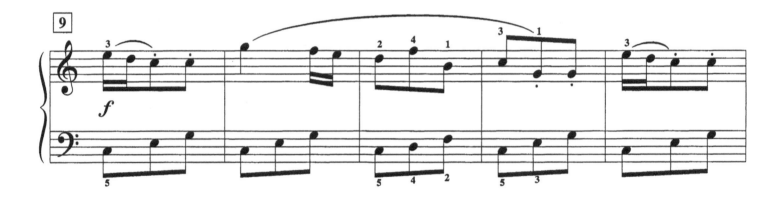

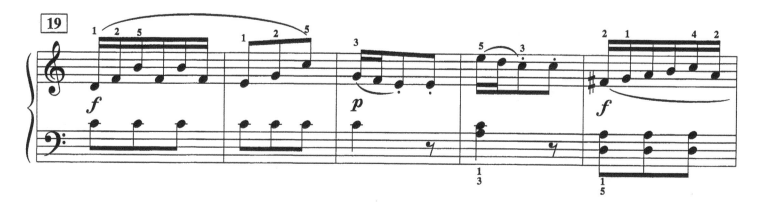

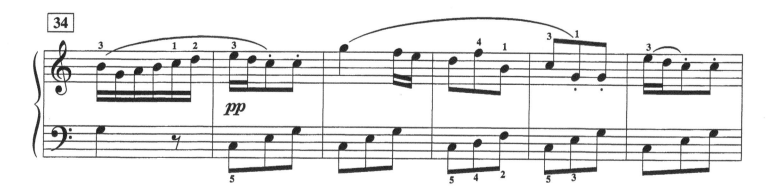

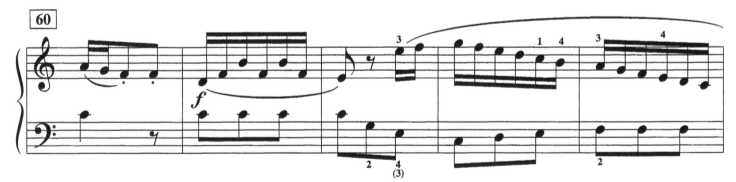

Exploring the Score: How many times is the opening 8-measure theme stated?

three times   four times   five times   *(circle one)*

Sonatina in A Minor

Russell Jacoby
(1949, U.S.)

Briskly, spirited

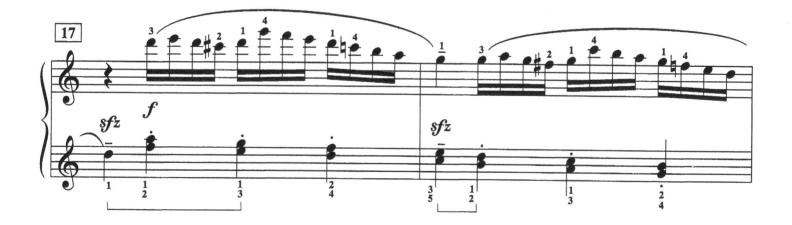

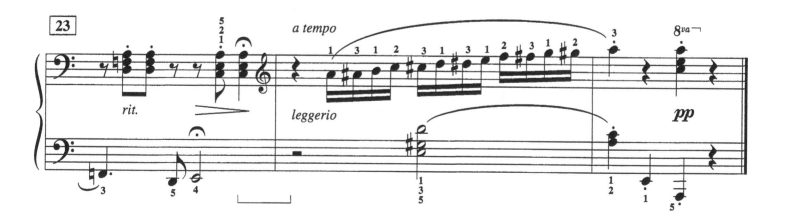

Sonatina in G

Jean T. Latour
(1766-1837)

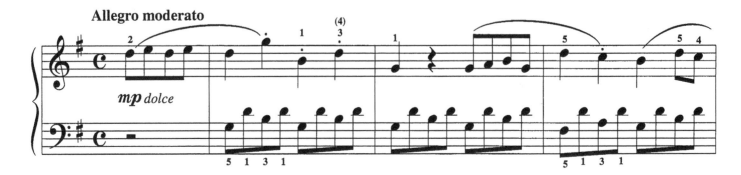

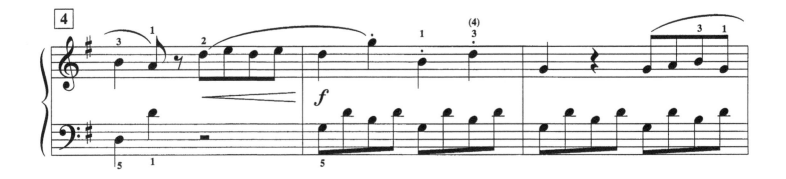

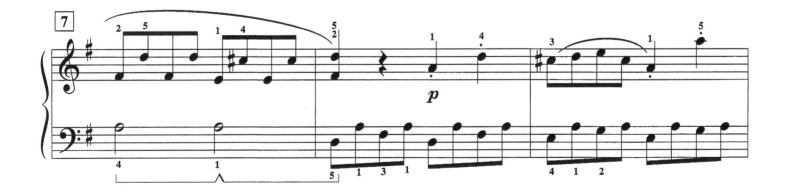

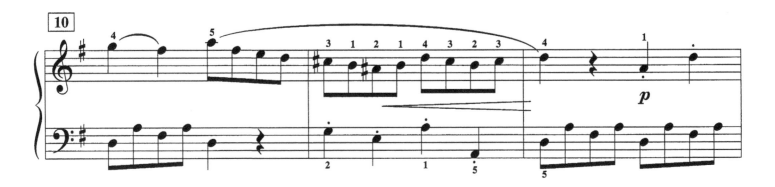

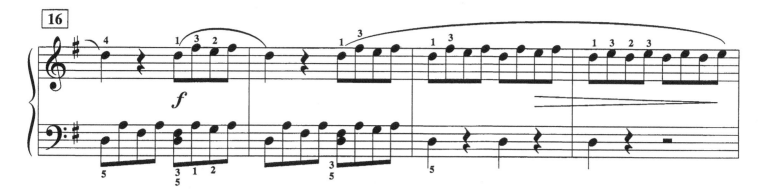

Exploring the Score: How would you label the music in measures 16-19?

           coda   2nd theme   transition

II

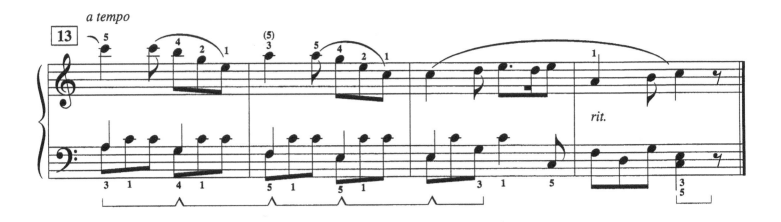

Exploring the Score: In what two ways does the 2nd line of music vary from the 1st line?

III

Theme

Moderato

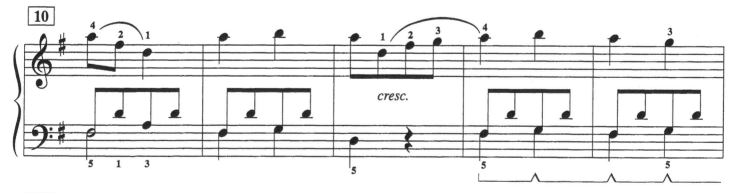

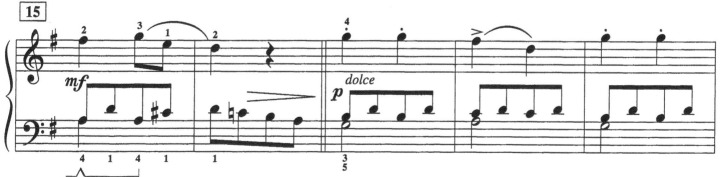

Exploring the Score: What is the form of the Theme? _____ It is presented using:

    ♩'s and **8th notes**   ♩'s and **triplets**   ♩'s and **16th notes**   *(circle one)*

Variation 1

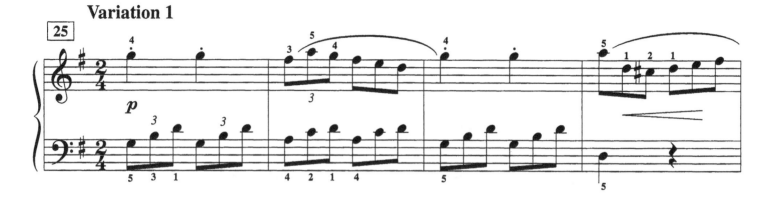

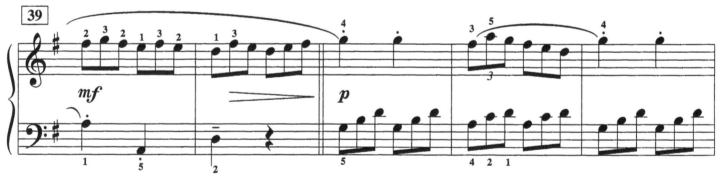

Exploring the Score: Is the form of Variation 1 the same as the form of the Theme? _____

Variation 1 is presented using:

♩'s and **8th notes**   ♩'s and **triplets**   ♩'s and **16th notes**   *(circle one)*

Variation 2

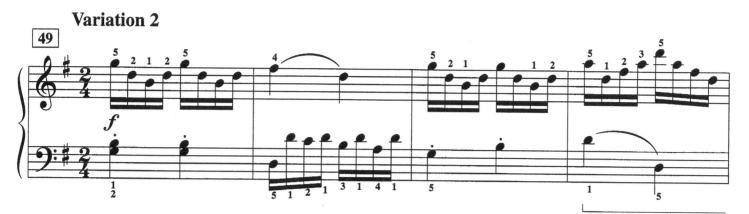

Exploring the Score: Is the form of Variation 2 the same as the form of the Theme? _____

Variation 2 is presented using:

♩'s and **8th notes**   ♩'s and **triplets**   ♩'s and **16th notes**   *(circle one)*

FF1111

Sonatina
Op. 157, No. 1

Fritz Spindler
(1817-1905)

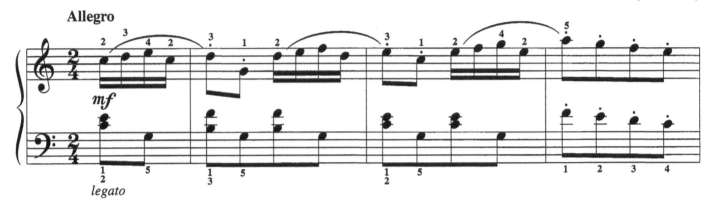

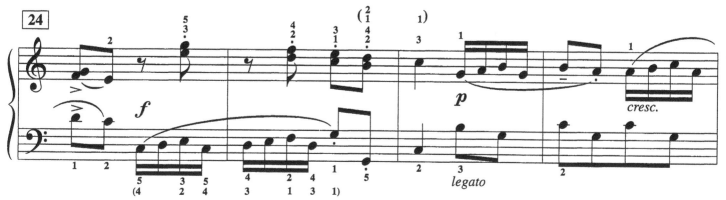

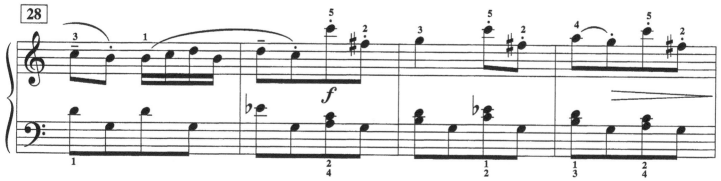

Exploring the Score: This piece is in binary form. ‖: **A** :‖‖: **B** :‖

Instead of having the usual repeat signs, however, each section
is written out twice: **A A B B**

• Label each **A section** and each **B section** in your music.

II

Tarantella

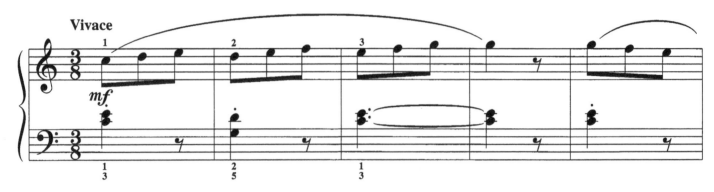

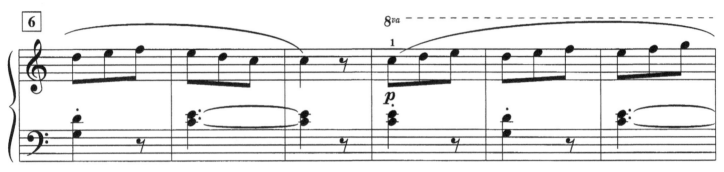

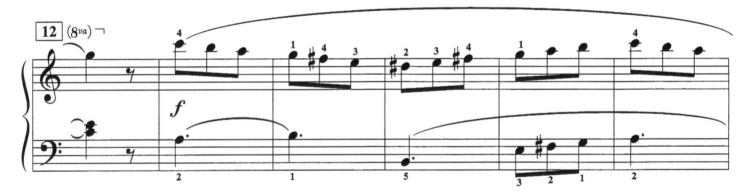

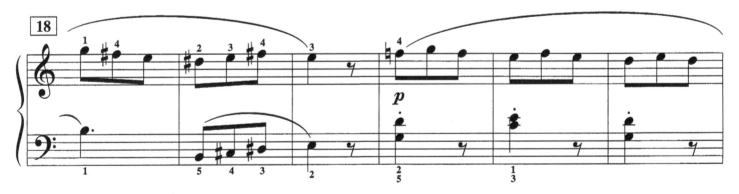

53

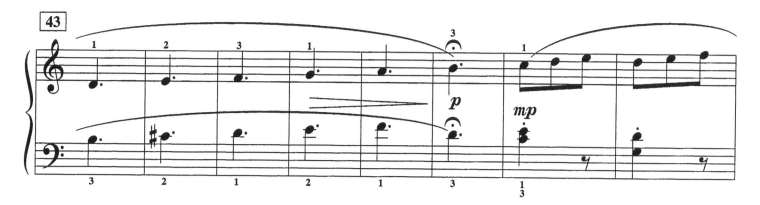

FF1111

Exploring the Score: Which fermata precedes (comes before) the return of the opening theme?

⌢ the fermata at *measure 48*   ⌢ the fermata at *measure 62*   (*circle one*)

Sonatina
Op. 55, No. 1

Friedrich Kuhlau
(1786-1832)

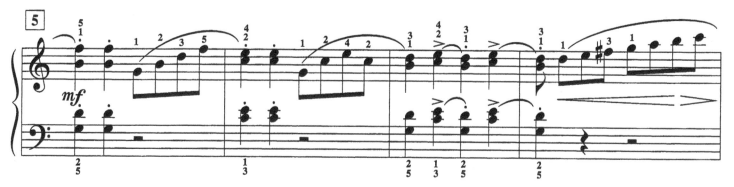

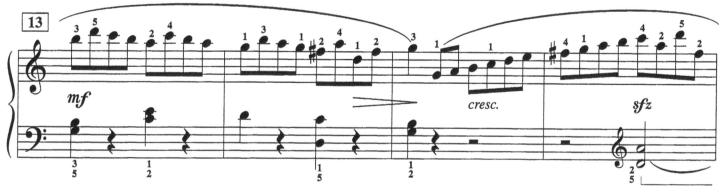

56

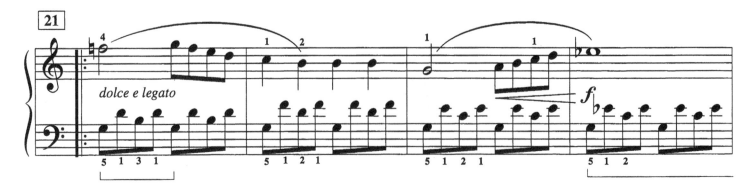

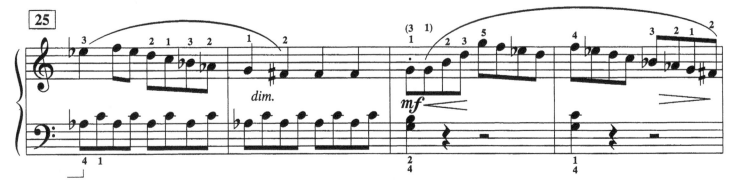

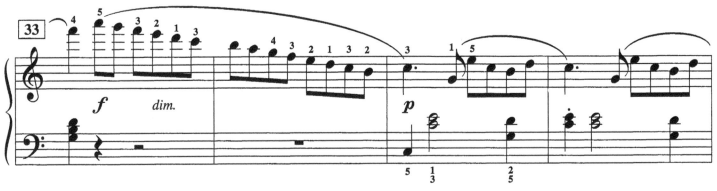

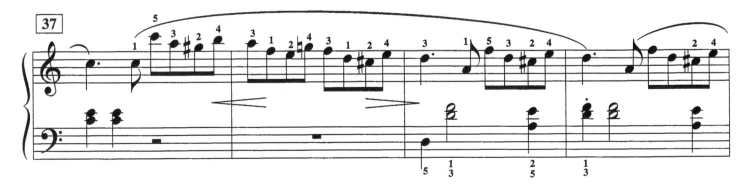

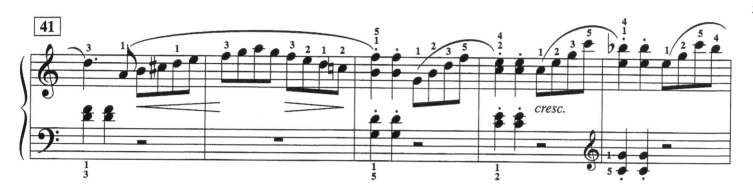

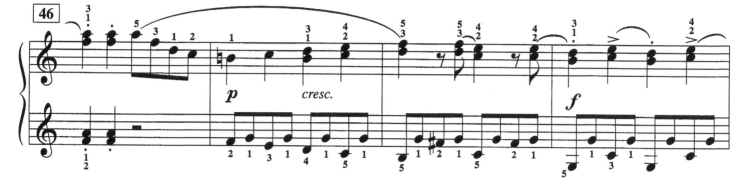

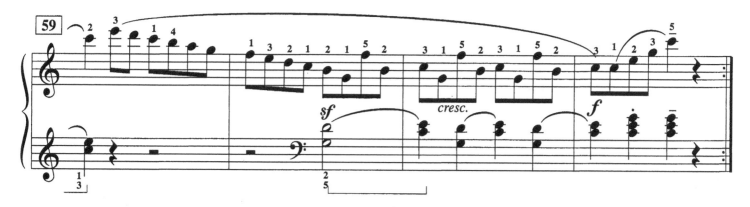

Exploring the Score: This movement is in **sonata-allegro form**. Review this important form
with your teacher, using page 5. Then mark the following in your music.

Exposition	Development	Recapitulation
1st theme		1st theme
2nd theme (in the dominant)		2nd theme (in tonic)
closing theme		closing theme

58

II

Vivace

FF1111

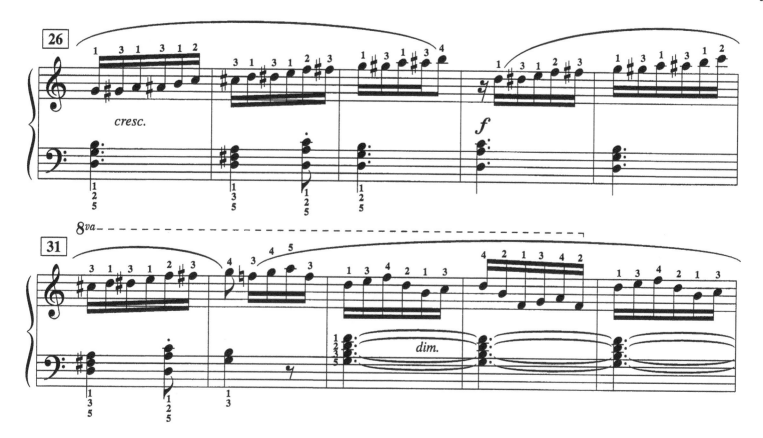

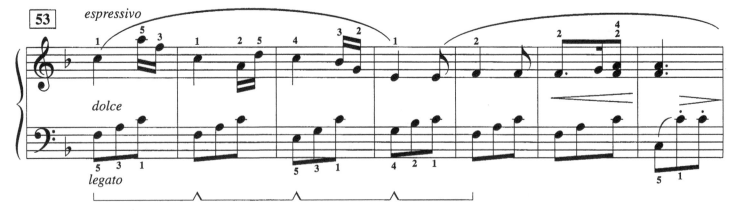

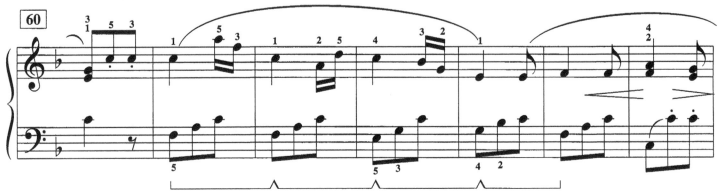

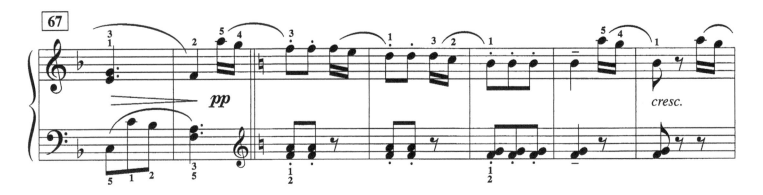

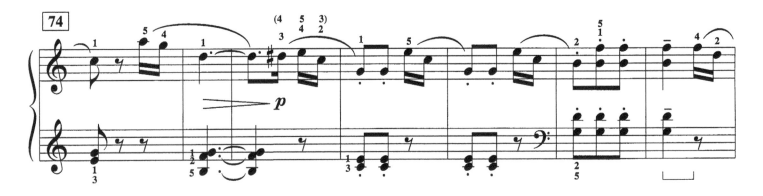

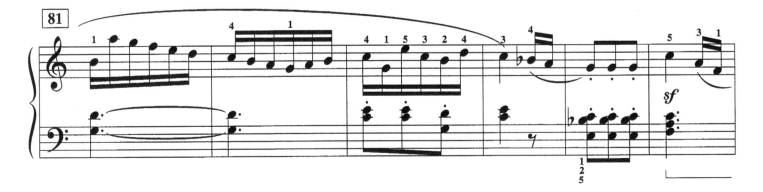

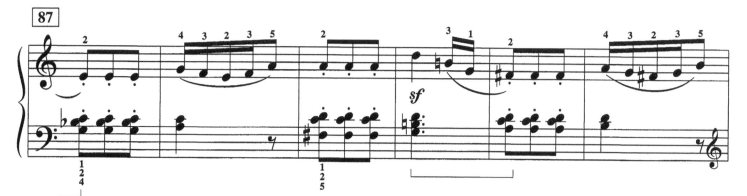

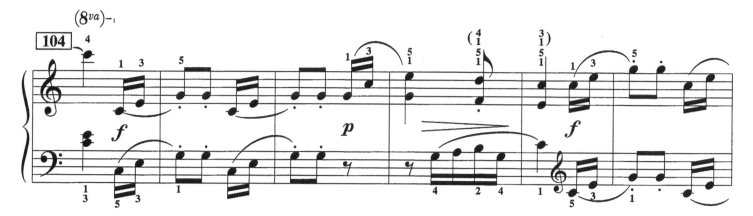

Exploring the Score: This movement is in rondo form: **A B A C A coda.**

With the help of your teacher, mark each section in your music.

DICTIONARY OF MUSICAL TERMS

Adagio	*Andante*	*Moderato*	*Allegretto*	*Allegro*	*Vivace*
slowly	walking tempo	moderate tempo	rather fast	fast	very fast

SIGN	TERM	DEFINITION
accel.	*accelerando*	Gradually play faster.
♩>	**accent**	Play this note louder.
	alla breve	Cut time. Short for $\frac{2}{2}$ time signature. The half note gets the beat. (Two half note beats per measure.)
	Alberti bass	A left hand accompaniment which outlines the notes of a chord using the pattern: bottom-top-middle-top. The *Alberti bass* was popularized during the Classic period.
	Allegro moderato	Moderately fast.
♪	*appoggiatura*	An ornament which looks like a grace note, but is played on the beat and shares the duration of the principal note. An appoggiatura resolves a dissonance to a consonance.
	arpeggio	Rolled chord. Play the notes of the chord one at a time, rapidly, from bottom to top.
	assai	Much. For example, *allegro assai* means "quite fast."
	a tempo	Return to the beginning tempo (speed).
	binary form	A musical form with 2 sections (section A and section B). Each section usually repeats. ‖: A :‖: B :‖
	coda	Ending section. (A short *coda* is called a *codetta*.)
◁	*crescendo (cresc.)*	Play gradually louder.
▷	*decrescendo*	Same as *diminuendo*.
▷	*diminuendo. (dim.)*	Play gradually softer. (Same as *decrescendo*.)
	dolce	Sweetly.
	dominant	Step 5 of the scale (indicated with the Roman numeral V).
	e	And (Italian). For example, *cresc. e rit.*
espr.	*espressivo*	Expressively.
⌢	*fermata*	Hold this note longer than usual.
fz	*forzando*	Forced, accented. Same as *sforzando*.
	giocoso	Humorously.
♪	**grace note**	A decorative note, written in small type with a slash through the stem. Grace notes are played quickly, usually before the main tone. (See also *appoggiatura*.)
	grazioso	Gracefully.
	legato	Played smoothly, connected.
	lento	Slow; slower than *Adagio*.
	leggiero	Light and nimble.

SIGN	TERM	DEFINITION
	minuetto	Italian for "minuet." A minuet is a stately dance in $\frac{3}{4}$ time.
	non tanto	Not too much.
	pastorale	A piece imitating the music of shepherds; usually in $\frac{6}{8}$ time.
	phrase	A musical idea. Think of a phrase as a "musical sentence." It is shown in the music with a slur, also called a phrase mark.
	poco	A little.
	poco a poco	Little by little.
rit.	*ritardando*	Gradually slow down.
	romanza	A lyrical (song-like) instrumental piece.
	rondo form	The form for a piece that has a recurring A section. Ex: A B A C A
	rounded binary form	Two-part form (**A B**) with a special feature: the theme from section A returns within section B. ‖ **A** ‖ **B** (A) ‖
	score	The written music.
sfz or *sf*	*sforzando*	A sudden strong accent.
	simile	Similarly. Continue in the same way (same pedaling, same use of staccato, etc.).
	slur	Connect the notes over or under a slur.
	sonata	An instrumental piece; usually with 3 movements.
	sonata-allegro form	A musical form commonly used for first movements. See page 5.
	sonatina	A little sonata.
	staccato	Play *staccato* notes detached; disconnected.
	subito	Suddenly. For example, *subito piano* means "suddenly soft."
	tarantella	A rapid $\frac{6}{8}$ composition. In folklore, the dance was said to cure the bite of a tarantula spider.
	tempo	The speed of the music.
ten.	*tenuto*	Hold the note its full value.
	tenuto mark	Hold this note its full value. Press gently into the key.
	ternary	A musical form with 3 sections: **A B A**.
	theme	Melody. A piece may have several themes.
	theme and variations	A musical form which states a musical idea (theme) followed by modified presentations of the theme (variations). The variations may change the rhythm, harmony, time signature, etc.
	transition	A passage which connects two sections.
tr	**trill**	A quick repetition of the principal note with the note above it. (The number and speed of the repetitions depends on the music.)

ABOUT THE COMPOSERS

Thomas Attwood (1765-1838)

Attwood was an English organist and composer. He studied with Mozart who wrote teaching pieces for him. Attwood was co-founder and conductor of the London Philharmonic Society.

Ludwig van Beethoven (1770-1827)

Beethoven is one of the most well-known composers in history. He was born in Germany and studied with Haydn in Vienna. In spite of severe hearing loss which began in his mid 20's, Beethoven was a prolific composer. He even composed when totally deaf, though the condition shortened his career as a performer and conductor. His works include: 9 symphonies, 32 piano sonatas, 5 piano concertos, numerous chamber works, instrumental works, a ballet, an opera, other choral works, and 16 string quartets.

Muzio Clementi (1752-1832)

Clementi was a highly successful pianist and composer. He was born in Rome, educated in England, and toured widely throughout Europe. He established a publishing company and piano factory in England, and achieved lasting fame with his compositions and exercises for piano students.

Anton Diabelli (1781-1858)

A student of Haydn, Diabelli was a composer and music publisher in Vienna. His name is most often associated with the "33 Variations on a Theme by Diabelli" composed by Beethoven.

Tobias Haslinger (1787-1842)

Haslinger was a music publisher in Austria and a friend of Beethoven.

Russell Jacoby (1949-   )

Jacoby is an American composer, pianist and teacher. He has composed many chamber works and teaching pieces, intermediate to advanced.

Friedrich Kuhlau (1786-1832)

Kuhlau was born in Germany and spent most of his life as a court musician in Copenhagen. He wrote many piano pieces and compositions for flute.

Jean Theodore Latour (1766-1837)

(No information available.)

Frank Lynes (1853-1913)

Lynes was an American composer and organist who lived in Boston. He composed many piano teaching pieces for his students.

Fritz Spindler (1817-1905)

Spindler was a German pianist, composer, and very successful teacher. He is remembered for the piano pieces he wrote for his students.